The Haiku Blues
by Ted Becker and Patricia Lantz

WIPF & STOCK · Eugene, Oregon

Wipf and Stock Publishers
199 W 8th Ave, Suite 3
Eugene, OR 97401

The Haiku Blues
By Becker, Ted L. and Lantz, Patricia
Copyright©2015 by Becker, Ted L.
ISBN 13: 978-1-5326-3648-6
Publication date 6/30/2017
Previously published by Blurb, 2015

俳句 ブルース Haiku Blues

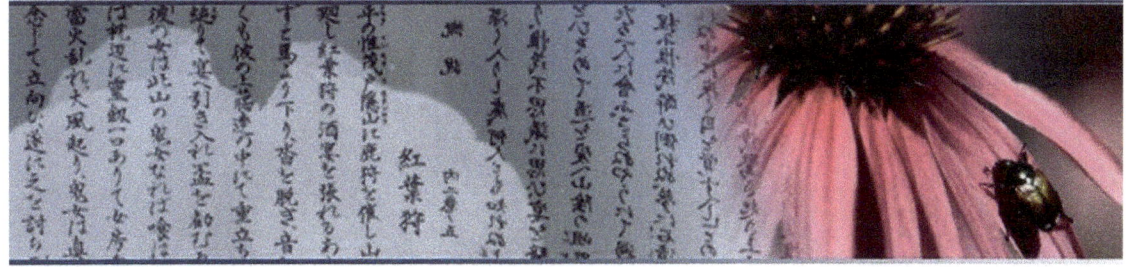

Join us on a spiritual journey through pain, love, life, places, politics, the realm of soul and for a few wry laughs.

We love the traditional Japanese haiku format of 17 syllables on 3 lines: 5-7-5. It is very symmetrical, terse and disciplined. The brevity forces one to think hard and deep to find the right word precisely in order to convey the feeling, insight and irony inside. Ancient haiku often trail off into space and leave it up to the reader to insert their own meaning into it. Haiku are designed to be interactive.

Our Haiku are meant to be interactive also. However, these are not your great grandfather's haiku. This is Modern American Haiku. We do keep the fundamental format, but that's all. For one thing, we give them titles, which we believe helps focus the reader on the punch in each haiku. Yes, they have a message in them, but it's open to the reader's interpretation and how it relates to their own personal experiences.

Second, there is word play. We like to rhyme. We like alliteration. We like puns. We think that the way we sprinkle these throughout the book helps one absorb the message better. Third, there is the extra dimension of the images in which many of the haiku are embedded or by which they are framed. We believe the reader will be amazed at how well the illustrations deepen the haiku and draw one back to the book.

Finally, the entire book is one Zen. It took 10 years to complete. We believe that the philosophy woven throughout the book is consistent with just about every religion in this world. All life in this world starts with pain and no one has ever known where it ends. Life on earth is a transit. This book is our transition. It shares our understanding of the world we have traversed and we hope that it helps each reader better understand or cope with their own.

Each haiku in our book is meant to be a meditative, sensory, feeling experience. You can't read them all at once. It may even take years before you come to your own deep understanding of what any mean to you, or the latent message appears.

You have not purchased a book, you've found a companion.

Ted Becker & Patricia Lantz

To Bob Dylan
Whose poetry inspires

Table of Contents

Introduction to The Haiku Blues

The Haiku Blues...10
The Anti-Muse...11
The Nature of Haiku...12
Basho's Last Poem...13

The Divorce Blues

Doomed From End to End...16
Our Fatal Flaw...17
Welcome to God's Penal Colony...18
It's not Alzheimer's, It's Adultery...19
Not the Best of Years...20
The Legion of the Zombies...21
Just Desserts?...22
Circus of the Cuckold...23
The Passion of Betrayal...24
See No Music...25
The Improbable Dream...26
The Goddess of Shattered Crystal...27
Wasted Love...28
Bad Karma...29
Forever Sore...30
Pure Love on Earth...31
Free to Choose Your Fate...32
You Can't Sink a Sunken Ship...33
Love May Not Conquer All...34
Men's Worst Heart Aches...35
Out of Service...37

Full Spectrum of Blue

The Full Spectrum of Blue...40
The Ocean's Obsession...41
Young Love...42
Smoke Sauna with Finnish Friends in Winter...43
Cooke Strait on a Wintery Day...44
Catching One at Point Panic...45
Chicago's Burning Question...46
Get Your Tix on Route 66...47
Redneck Riviera...48
Gray Sunset over Pensacola Bay...49
Chebeague Island...50
Dockside: Portland, Maine...51
The Lincoln Tunnel Symphony...52
Kyoto Stone Garden...53
When Gas Stations Were Service Stations...54
When America Worked...55
Springtime in Washington Square Park...56
The Class's 25th Year Reunion...57
New York City From Eagle Rock...58
Montauk Lighthouse...59
Big Time College Football...60
Baby Boomers as Grandparents...61
Beware of Acid Trips...62
Space Funerals...63
The Good Life on Radar...64
The Truth and Beauty Within...65

Table of Contents... cont.

We "Groundlings" at Shakespeare's Globe Theater... 66
Academy Awards Night... 67
Teacher to the Student... 68
Flower Dogs... 69
Draining Emotions... 70
The Internet As Pot... 71
Stormed... 72
Rap Music... 73
Lips are the Window of the Soul... 74
Starry Scary Night... 75
Wall Street Logic... 76
Telephone Hell... 77
The Everyday Space Launch... 78
Major Wipeout... 79
Even a Dead Man's Best Friend... 80
Eau De Doo Doo... 81
The Minute Symphony... 82
Pretty Poison, or She's a Venus Fly Trap... 83
Our Dark Universe... 84
Not Gitmo, Orgasma... 85
Pornication... 86
It's the Kiss... 87
Internet Dating... 88
Good and Bad Winds... 89

Two Squirrels and Their Nosy Neighbor... 91
(A Zen Poem of Many Haikus)

The Constitutional Blues

The Wrong Obsession... 107
The New 4th... 108
Myth America... 109
The Indian in Us All... 110
America's Genius... 111
California Dreaming... 112
American Politics: Ala Carte... 113
The American "Free" Press... 114
President Dubyah... 115
Free Enterprise... 116
The High and (not so) Mighty... 117
The American Legal Process... 118
The Late, Unlamented Right to Privacy... 119
The Childlike World of Geopolitics... 120
Fair Exchange... 121
Discount the Truth... 122
The "New" World Order... 123
The Bottom Line for Global Corporations... 124
Help Fight the U.S. Work Force... 125
The Final Stage of Imperialism... 126
The Looming Global Cataclysm... 127
If Only the Public Knew... 128
My Life as a Termite... 128
Where FDR Died and Lives... 130
The Democracy Gene... 131

Table of Contents... cont.

The Soul-Bendin' Blues

Soul-Mates are Fated or Never... 135
Dream On... 136
Seeing the Light... 137
Baptized at 72... 138
God's Retrievers... 139
Blood Twilights... 140
Heavenly Missions... 141
Only God Hears... 142
How to Avoid a Deadly Sin... 143
Sexual Spirituality... 144
When God Smiles and Sighs... 145
Lucky in Life... 146
In the Wake of Rapture... 147
Will You Like What You See... 148
Flying Out... 149
Brighter is Lighter... 150
Good Way to Go... 151
To My Alter Ego in a Parallel Universe... 152
Soul Survivors... 153

Alone on the Bridge of Gratitude... 155
(A Zen Poem of Many Haikus)

Finale... 169
(in 7 Zenned Haikus)

The Haiku Blues

I write haiku when
I'm feelin' blue and when love and
pain make me want to.

The Anti-Muse

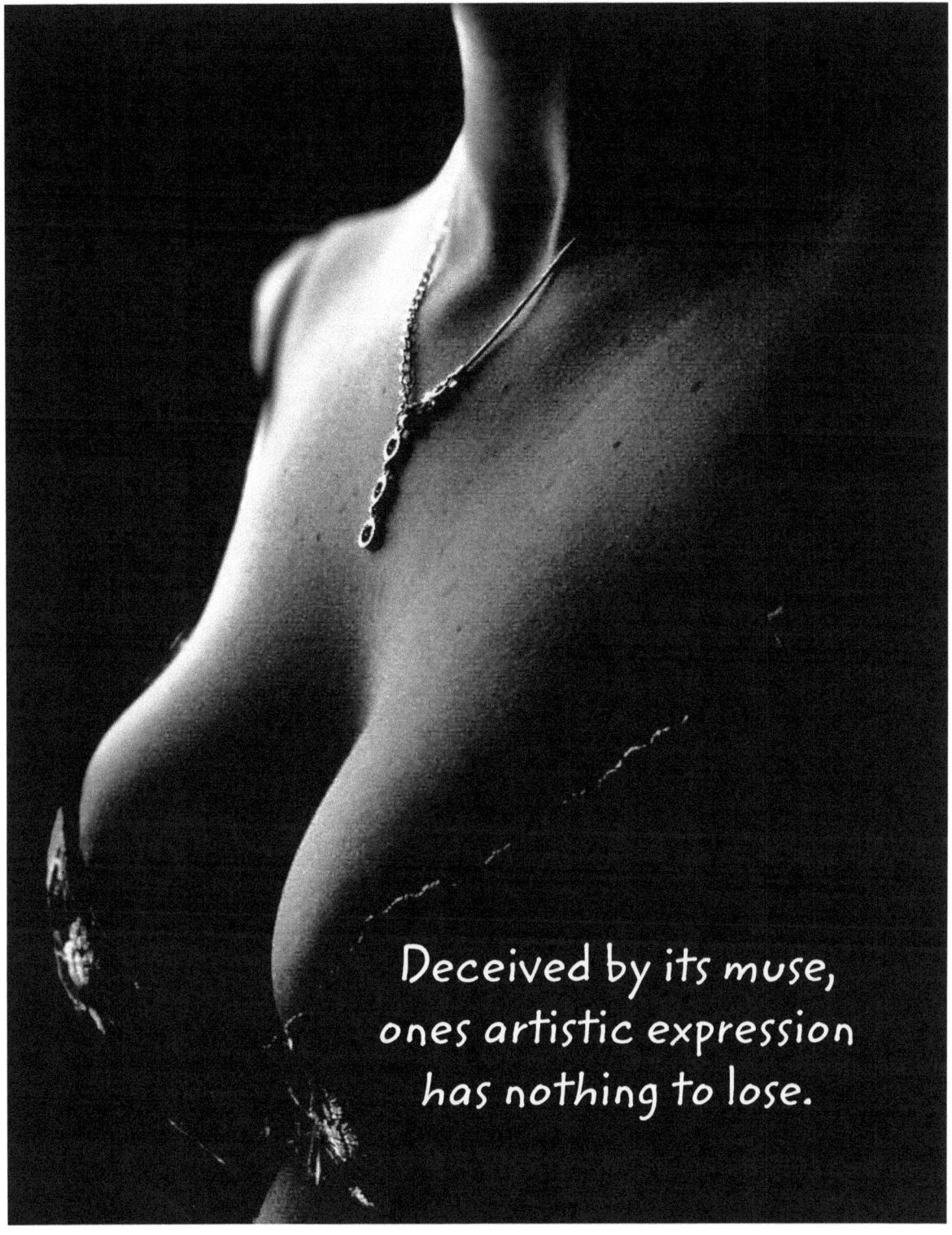

Deceived by its muse, ones artistic expression has nothing to lose.

The Nature of Haiku

Haiku sees nature
as a waterfall that drowns,
and restores our souls.

Basho's Last Poem

He wrote no last poem
because each was the sunburst
that never ended.

Doomed From End to End

Any rifts before
you wed won't be healed in bed
or sealed 'til one's dead.

Our Fatal Flaw

You were right from the start. We were imperfect. Our one defect was us.

Welcome to God's Penal Colony

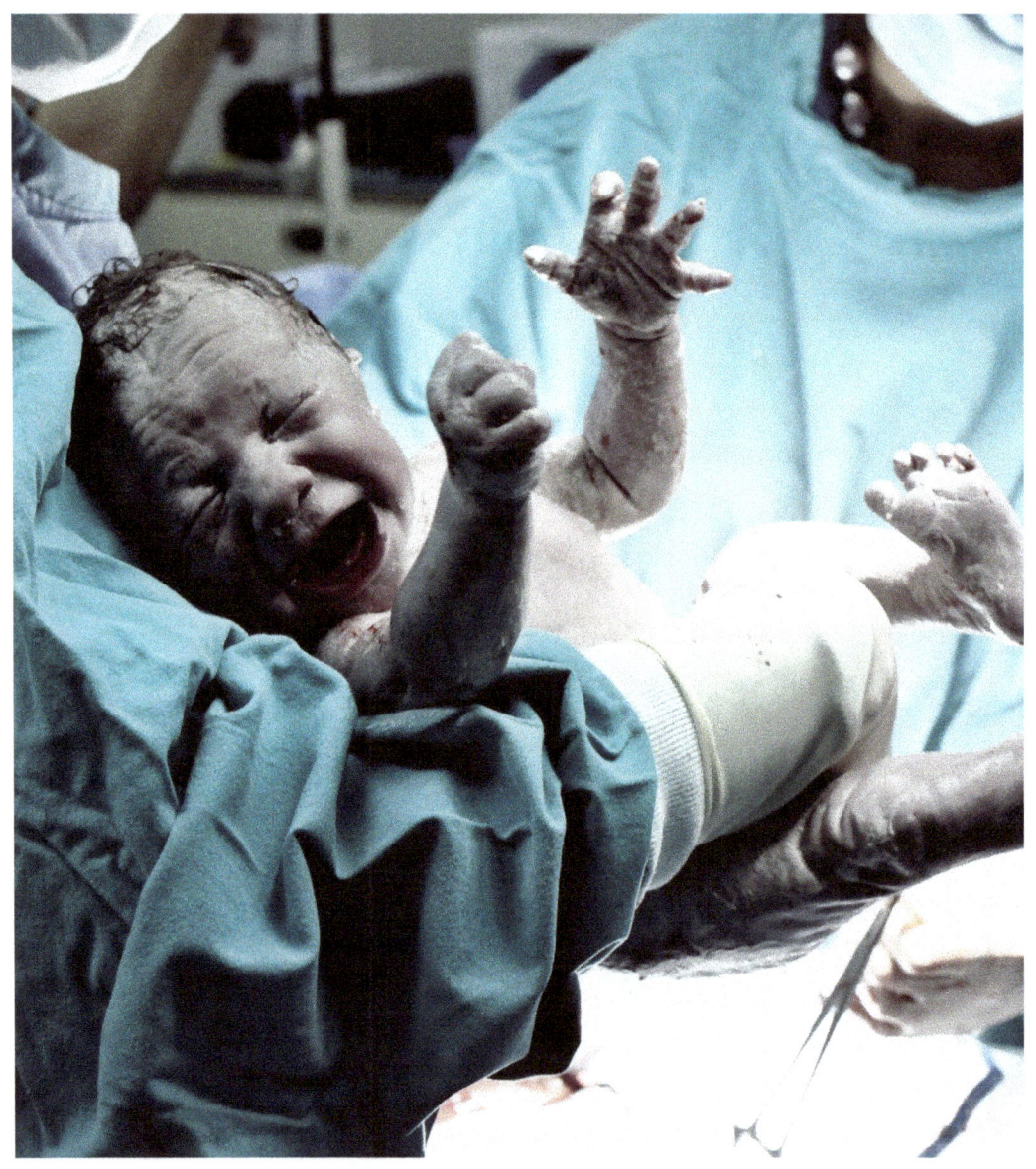

No wonder babes cry
when birthed to this world of hurt.
Their sentence is life.

It's Not Alzheimer's, It's Adultery

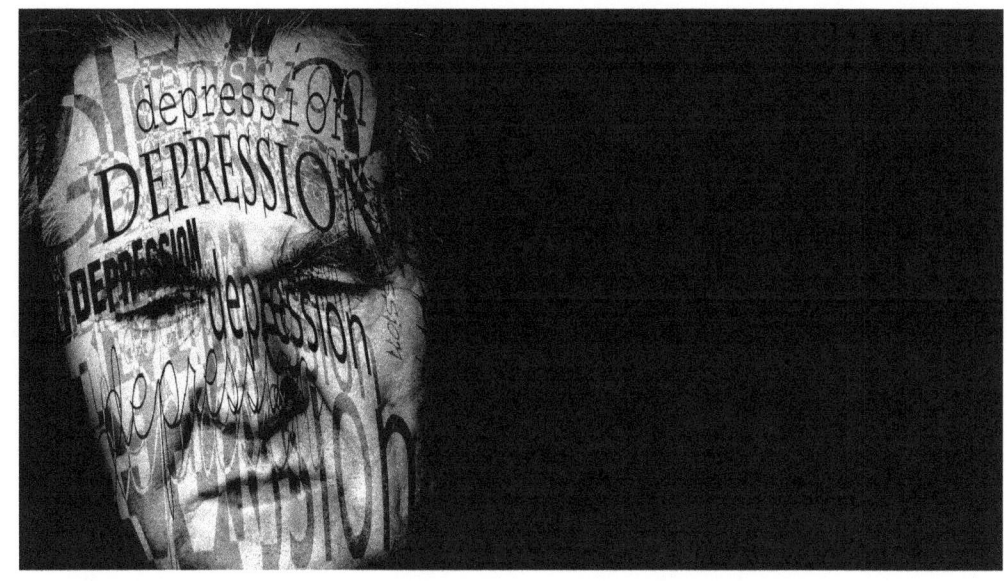

Mumbling to yourself,
shaking your head. Mind crumbling,
stumbling into dread.

Not the Best Years

My hip displaced, my
hope erased. My self effaced.
Sacred words disgraced.

The Legion of Zombies

Cored by cheating wives
they march numbed, with hollowed center
yearning for new lives.

Just Desserts?

Marriages thrilled with licit lechery may spur wicked treachery.

The Circus of the Cuckold

Steep roller coasters,
bungees, high wire and just you:
clown, freak show and dirt.

The Passion of Betrayal

Stabbed in my heart and crowned by thorns, Caesar, Jesus, betrayal gores us.

See No Music

What happens to chords
when blinded trust makes us tone
deaf to harmony?

The Improbable Dream

She changed my ways. I
stopped my stuff and cheered her up,
but not far enough.

The Goddess of Shattered Crystal

I gave the Goddess
my true love, a crystal heart.
One day she dropped it.

Wasted Love

Pure love lavished on
ingrates is like spilt fine wine
or pearls before swine

Salvator Rosa (Italian, 1615 - 1673) PD-art

Bad Karma

William Blake. La escala de Jacob. 1799-07

To exact revenge
is poor advice: bad karma
is its own device.

Forever Sore

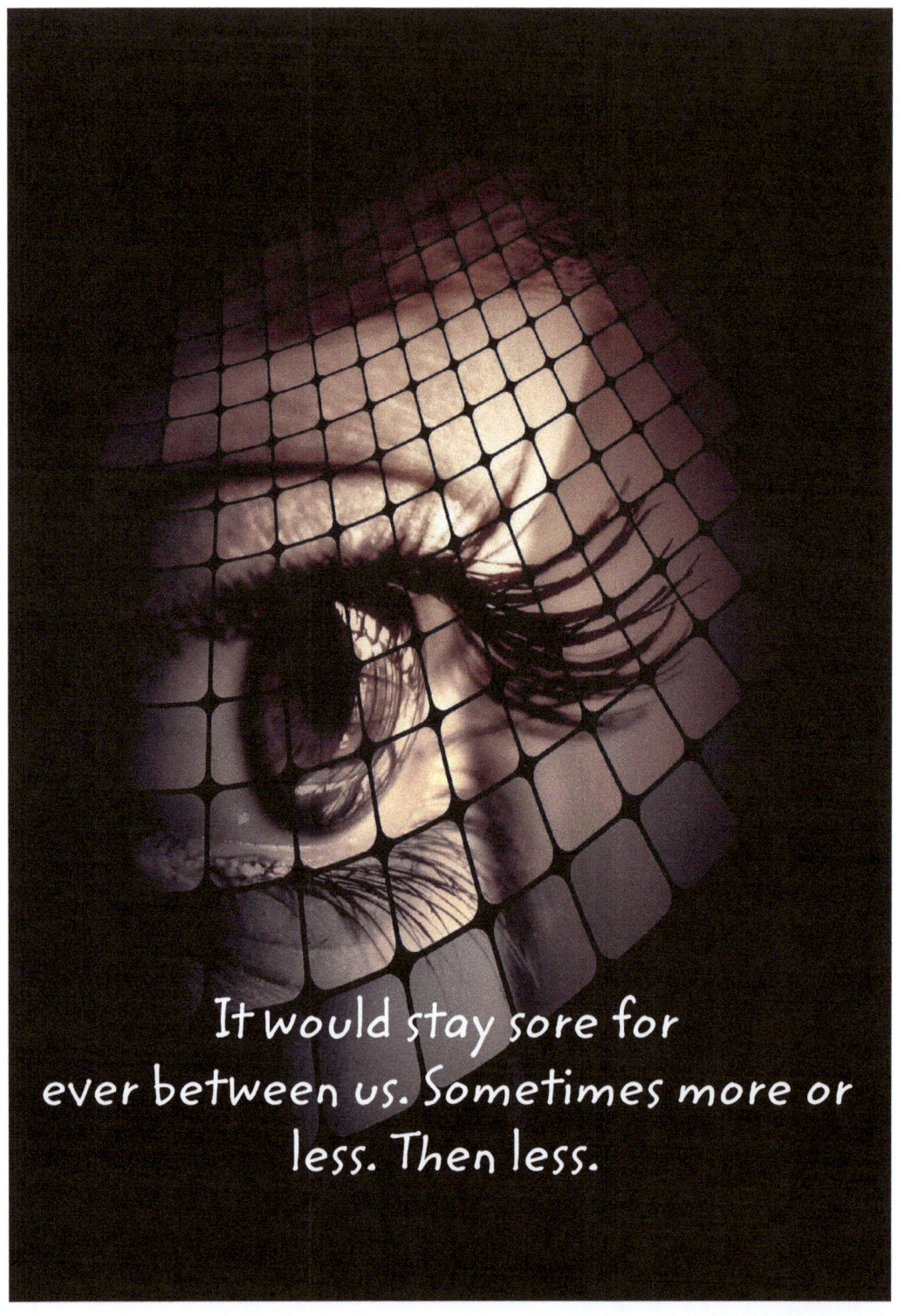

Pure Love on Earth

The only pure love
you'll find on this wretched orb
is your dog's for you.

Free to Choose Your Fate

I freely chose those paths I felt best for me. The rest was destiny.

You Can't Sink a Sunken Ship

Say your worst, droll or manic—you're a depth charge that hit the Titanic.

Love May Not Conquer All

Love is rich, but not omnipotent. It can go broke, even well spent.

Men's Worst Heart Aches

Putting down the dog
of their life, putting up with
women's memories.

Out of Service

Twenty five years
of hauling tons of love,
swathed in sweat.
In return, one small bundle.

Countless instances
of giving in for the sake of peace
on matters of substance.
In return: unrelenting grudges.

Endless negotiation
on how to do or not do that
and self alterations.
In return: a constant spat.

Thousands of breakfasts
catering to her special tastes
though her appetite waned,
they never seemed a waste.

Absorbing complaints
about sexism in the world of work
and unfair restraints.
They weighed heavily on me.

Offering advice
on potential pitfalls and traps
always met with fierce resistance.
Interpreted as interference.

I understand why you shy from me
and I seem to make you nervous.
It's true she committed adultery,
and that put me- out of service.

The Full Spectrum of Blue

The Full Spectrum of Blue

Slate, navy, baby,
royal, aqua, light and deep.
I got all them blues.

The Ocean's Obsession

Seas don't care about wars, wrecks, quakes or typhoons. They only love the moon.

Young Love

Fiery, seminal,
consuming our lives. Too bad
it's ephemeral.

Smoke Sauna with Finnish Friends in Winter

Searing dry heat, smoke enhanced, we sit entranced, baked, admiring the ice.

Cooke Strait on a Wintery Day

Cook Strait, New Zealand (1884)Oil by Nicholas Chevalier (1828 - 1902) ((PD-art))

Horizontal rain:
bone chilling and so thrillng
it hardboils your brain.

Catching One at Point Panic

Through the spray, in the
curl, down the face. "Hey br'ah, you're
in da 'locals' place."

Chicago's Burning Question

Why don't iced flakes on
my lashes melt from the red
hot cold up my nose?

Get Your Tix on Route 66

From Chi to L.A.
the heartland lies bleeding. Me?
Thrice stopped for speeding.

Redneck Riviera

Fine sand and cheese grits, lots of Suthin' drawl...top guns on bikini trawl.

Gray Sunset over Pensacola Bay

Dark green silhouettes
sliced by silver and pewter
slivers of water.

Chebeague Island

Horns groan through the mist,
ferried to lobsterman's isle
where time laps us up.

Dockside: Portland, Maine

Creaking boards, storied
masts, working town with docks kissed
by years gone too fast.

The Lincoln Tunnel Symphony

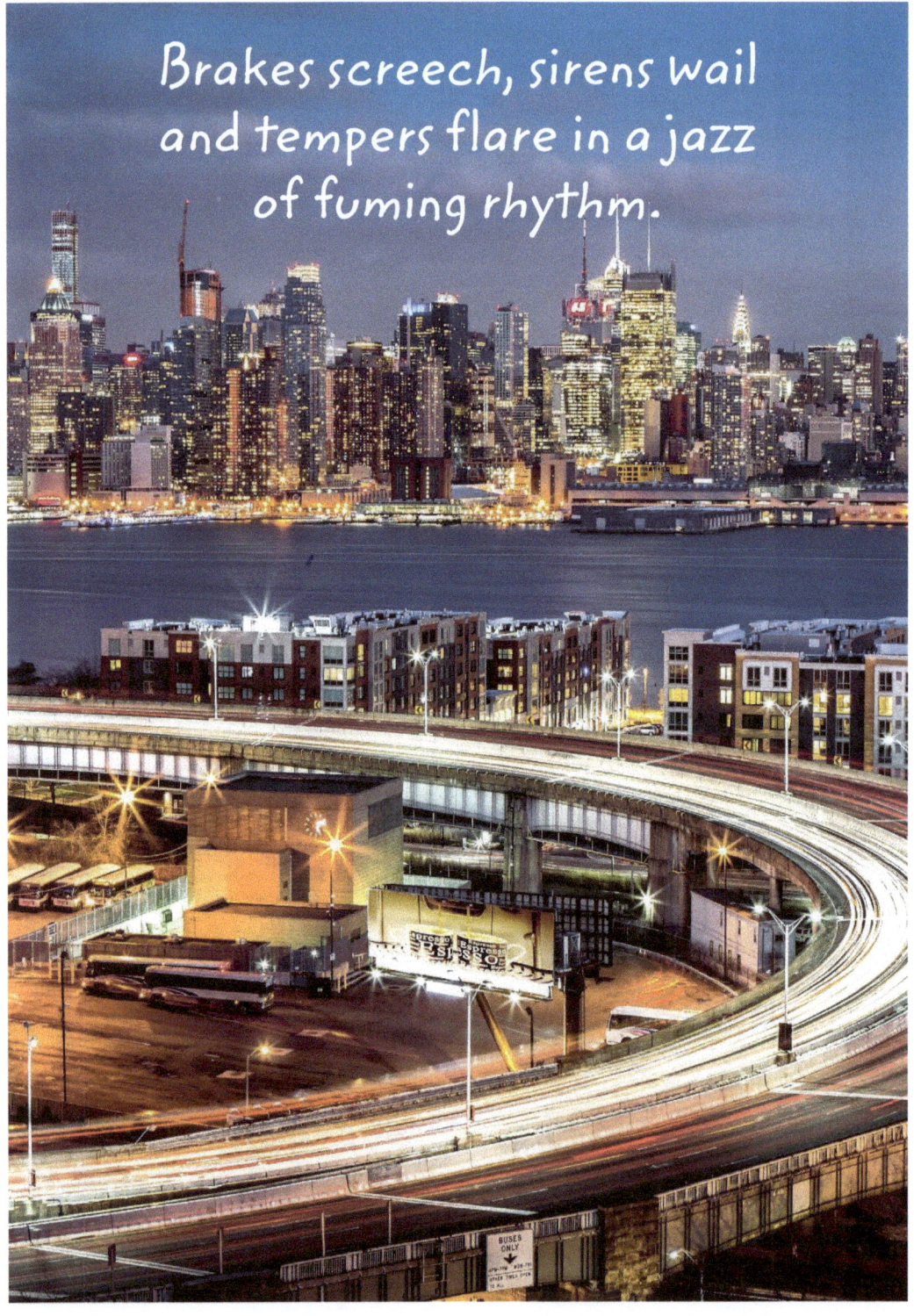

Brakes screech, sirens wail and tempers flare in a jazz of fuming rhythm.

Kyoto Stone Garden

I contemplate the
stones arranged to atone for
my pilgrimage there.

When Gas Stations Were Service Stations

Your tires need air. You
need oil. I'll clean your windshield.
Now? Pump your own gas.

When America Worked

Doc's home calls, service stations, milk delivered: When America worked.

Springtime in Washington Square Park

The Class's 25th Year Reunion

New York City From Eagle Rock

Long jagged ridge of
sharp mesas and peaks piercing
a blue skyed mirror.

Montauk Lighthouse

Staid, staunch sentinel,
gallant guard of mystic nights,
watched us slip on rocks.

Big Time College Football

Pro ball in college
ranks, while boards hoard endowments
and let learning tank.

Baby Boomers as Grandparents

They blew past their kids,
wanting too much. As grannies,
they're getting to touch.

Beware of Acid Trips

Seconds take hours, lush
hues, intense awe. "Yo, dude! You
broke the friggin' law."

Space Funerals

Orbiting corpses:
future bugs scrunched to mush on
alien windshields.

The Good Life on Radar

Don't be a blip or false echo. The trick's being a real UFO.

The Truth and Beauty Within

Those who trek endless ranges and seek perfect views must do them within.

We "Groundlings" at Shakespeare's Globe Theater

Acted upon, we
are drawn to ancient wisdom
as though we were then.

Academy Awards Night

Struttin' at the Ritz, puttin' on the glitz, while the Devil leers and drools.

Teacher to the Student

Maroon Bells ~ Aspen, Colorado
Photographer, Holt Lantz

Are you a fountain-
gushing, spouting, quenching? No,
you are a mountain.

Flower Dogs

Mate German Shepherds and Pomeranians. You'll breed: Geraniums.

Draining Emotions

When grief sinks into
my cortex, the only way out's
that luring vortex.

The Internet As Pot

Timespace dissolve.
Absolutely self-involved.
Can't move. I'm evolved! and

Stormed

Annihilation!
All is savaged. Tarnation!
My home is ravaged!

Rap Music

Lips are the Window of the Soul

Having a mean smirk
on your mug means you're a jerk
and likely a thug.

Starry Scary Night

Wall Street Logic

Greed, fear, and despair: the 'rational' motives of wild-eyed bulls and bears.

Telephone Hell

Beep beep boop beep boop.
"You're in Telephone Hell. Thanks for waiting." Beep boop.

The Everyday Space Launch

As elevator's doors close, glazed eyes gaze into cubed space. All minds doze.

Major Wipeout

Over the falls: drubbed,
maytagged, sandbagged and hard scrubbed—
grope through foam to air.

Even a Dead Man's Best Friend

Dogs sniffing rubble
need long rests. Human remains
make them too depressed.

Eau De Doo Doo

Rolling in horse dung
is something dogs do. To them
it's perfume for you.

The Minute Symphony

A man and woman who meshed perfectly, but for the blink of an eye.

Pretty Poison, or She's a Venus Fly Trap

Sumptuous beauty's
allure locks dumb preys into
her lethal embrace.

Our Dark Universe

Dark energy, dark matter, black holes everywhere: Human history.

Not Gitmo, Orgasma

Screams, shrieks, moans and groans, simpering and whimpering. Gitmo? Orgasma!

Pornication

Nude, lewd, erotic,
exotic. Starved lust aroused
by thoughts Quixotic.

It's the Kiss

Sex for hire, or love
for money. It's a choice, but
it's the kiss, honey.

Internet Dating

Internet dating's like panning for gold: Lots of sand; little to hold.

Good and Bad Winds

Light, trade, sea breezes,
gusty, squally, gales, monsoons,
typhoons, old man's wheeze.

Two Squirrels and Their Nosy Neighbor

I.

A pair of squirrels
dwell in an old poplar tree
that lives next to me.

II.

A gnarled, pocked dome is
cupping a charcoal hole in
which they make their home.

III.

I know much about them but they have little sense of my existence.

IV.

My eyes catch their swift
darts and frenzied capers for
their nosy neighbor.

V.

While they are playmates, mostly they are alone to say to each their own.

VI.

Hunched on haunches,
crunching, munching, and nibbling
they suddenly launch.

VII.

When a large moving
creature appears on their screen,
aloft they careen.

VIII.

Up the trunk, from limb
to twig...they bound...twig to branch
to trunk, back to ground.

IX.

Sometimes they chatter
and tail each other until
it doesn't matter.

X.

In night's dark I can't
see whether together they may
be huddled, cuddled.

XI.

Animal selves feel
safe, in some hollow, rooted,
never to exit.

The Constitutional Blues

The Wrong Obsessions

Your were sent here for good reason
but given little information.
To those few who pass through, it's a brief season
in their spirit's transformation.

What little play you have in life
you must stoke love's flame from birth.
Despite all you gain from work and strife,
it's the only thing you take from Earth.

For whatever cause, if it gets extinguished,
the consequence is utter devastation.
All that's left for you is latent anguish
over your next reincarnation.

So, if this sad world is where you want to be
then wallow in your possessions.
The next time around you may come to see
You were the author of the wrong obsessions.

The New 4th of July

Lustrous words of yore
dimmed by fireworks, silenced by
bluster, now a bore.

Myth America

It's boasting we're just,
"democratic" and lawful
that makes our wars grate.

"Forgotten Founders"

Splattered, scattered and battered, their culture endures, and beckons to us.

America's Genius

Luring brains over
business lanes-Europe's, Asian
and those screwed by Spain.

California Dreaming

Where our "manifest destiny" shoulda stopped and our future flip flopped.

American Politics: Ala Carte

Vintage whines, followed by baloney wrapped in ham. For dessert: Trifles

The American "Free" Press

Grand illusions of
ruthless media spinning
truthless conclusions.

President Dubyah

Snide shill for the slick
Dick on top. Sick politics
of the photo-op.

Free Enterprise

Victims of Laissez-Faire: isolated, selfish, bare: Hapless meals for wolves

The High and (not so) Mighty

High strife, high tech, high life, prep schooled, low piety, high anxiety.

The American Legal System

Two-tiered, much feared, too long, incomprehensible, indispensable.

The Late, Unlamented Right to Privacy

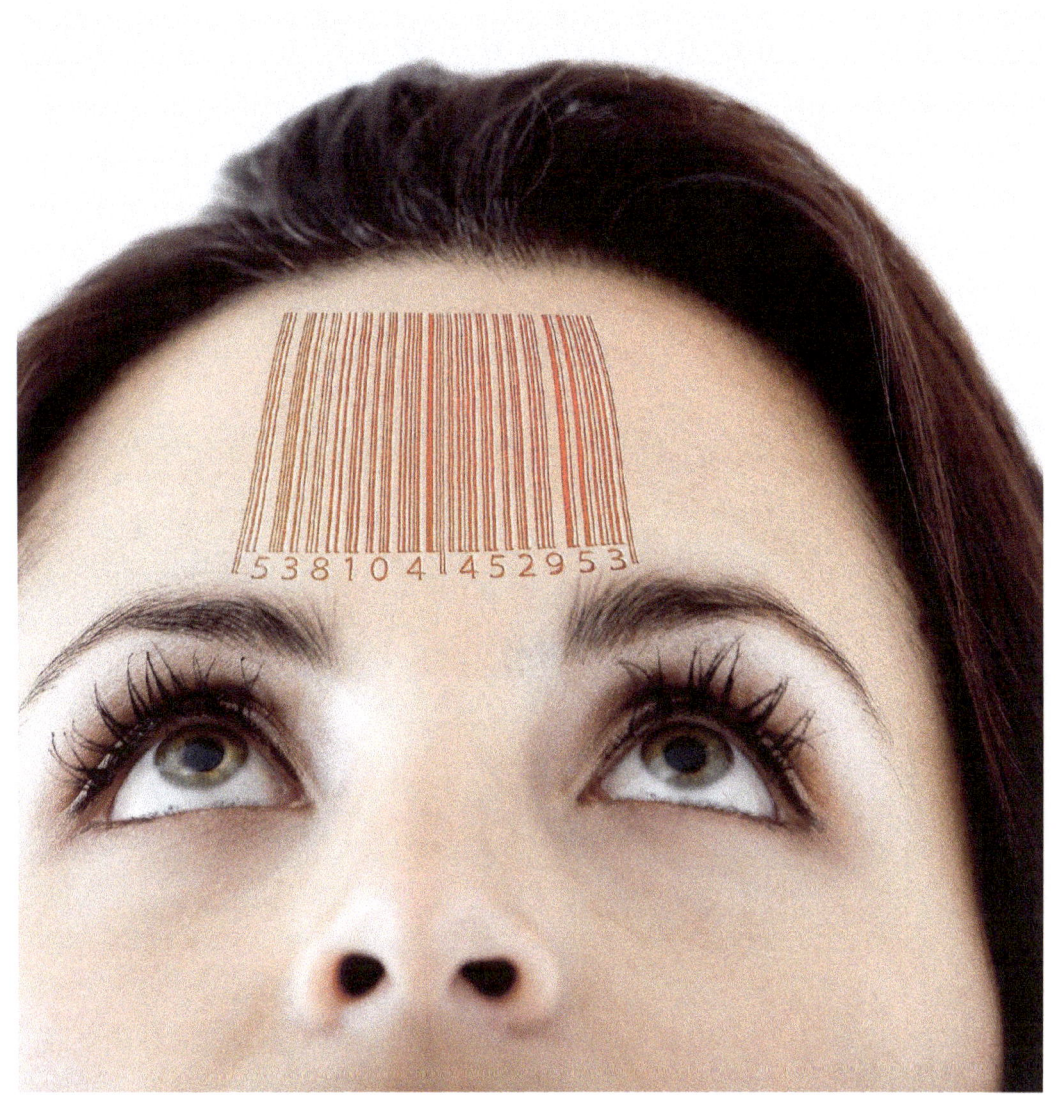

Bar codes in the brain,
scanners in the sky. Yourself?
Repealed by Congress

The Childlike World of Geopolitics

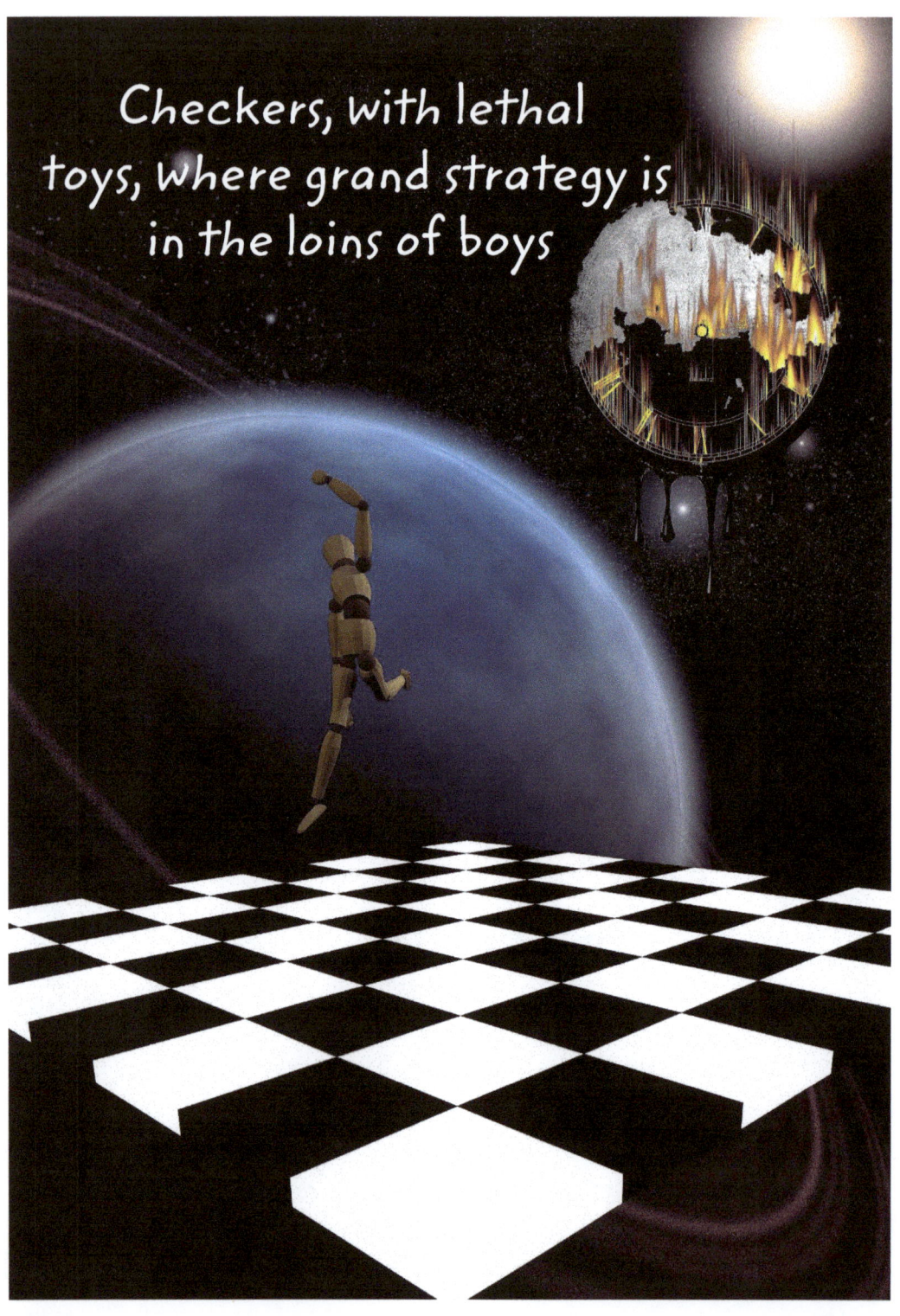

Fair Exchange

Canucks go south for
less taxed frills, while Yanks head north
for much cheaper pills.

Discount the Truth

Elections are not referenda. They are "sales" of hidden agendas.

The "New" World Order

IMF, World Bank, and NATO, madmen puffed with power. So what's new?

The Bottom Line for Global Corporations

Soil dispoilers, air polluters, tax evaders, traitors to nations.

Help Fight the U.S. Work Force

Stock values equal a
rigged Dow, union busting, jobs
to Asia. Buy now!

The Final Stage of Imperialism

The Looming Global Cataclysm

Catastrophe is Gaia's immunity: To cure our infection.

If Only the Public Knew

Until the people
are involved, global issues
will go unresolved.

My Life as a Termite

Gnawing away at rotten foundations fills me with good vibrations.

Where FDR Died and Lives

Time warp: Wry smile when death struck, still there. Such a small home for a giant.

The Democracy Gene

Those who empower others aren't heretics. It's their genetics.

The Soul-Bendin' Blues

Soul-Mates are Fated or Never

I

All my life I've been craving
someone to love and understand me,
a person to sense the me within me
and conjoin us with certainty.

There is a charge that breeds inside
that longs to fuse together,
to dissolve what keeps us apart
and infuse with the other.

It's not mere loneliness that drives us
but something above our humanity,
an urge to purge the self
that borders on insanity.

II

At times, in life, one believes
they've found an exception to the rule,
some kindred spirit who relieves
the dread of not being dual.

But soul-mates are hard to come by
on this solitary planet,
they come as often as a fly-by
of deep space icy comet.

You're not promised an Edenic garden
when your sown here on Earth,
so why's it so hard to harden
to the truth of such dearth.

Why keep demanding that human love
transcend the borders of the flesh?
You may as well command wings of doves
to become strands of golden mesh.

III

Yet there are such special soul-mates
but finding them is not our place.
If we're lucky enough to get one
it comes through other-world grace.

They are not sent to make us joyful
or to keep us calm in stress.
They come to make us peaceful
and help our soul progress.

But it won't be what you thought
because it's beyond our imaginations.
It will deluge your drought
and lead to unknown destinations.

So don't pine for human soul-mates,
one whose persona dies.
If you're granted one in a lifetime,
it's fate, and a soulful surprise.

Dream On

Choose a soul-mate for life and hereafter? That roar's celestial laughter.

Seeing the Light

Sparkling ripples in a light stream into me through a seam in the air.

Baptized at 72

I chose baptism
in my dotage, not as faith,
but for my homage.

God's Retrievers

Millie and Cape May Sunset, Photograph by Shary Skoloff

Golden love, a heart
wiser than her tongue, doggone
good at fetching souls.

Blood Twilights

Translucent glow, low in blood sky. Awesome, apt end to a day or life.

Heavenly Missions

Not coincidence.
A chance to play God's angel,
granted by request.

Only God Hears

Snob balls, tax write-offs, named halls. True charity, like prayer, flows easily.

How to Avoid a Deadly Sin

Be not proud of what's achieved, just grateful for its intended purpose.

Sexual Spirituality

Orgasmic fireworks. Imploding chasms. Two out of body bodies.

When God Smiles and Sighs

When we poke fun at ourselves, God smiles. When we mock others, She just sighs.

Lucky in Life

Life self-realized and with no regrets, is as lucky as it gets.

In the Wake of Rapture

Best yield from here with sorrow, not blame. Please save me from this place again.

Will You Like What You See?

Your life may flash in
your eyes before you die and
you should want to look.

Flying Out

Some die with loved ones grieving by, others leave with God alone, to fly.

Brighter is Lighter

The brighter is your incandescence, the lighter is your transcendence.

Good Way to Go

When death is near, if you can leave ecstatic, you'll avoid all traffic.

To My Alter Ego in a Parallel Universe

My mirror image
life's exquisite. When mine on
Earth cracks, I'll visit.

Soul Survivors

It's the survival
of our souls that means the most.
Bodies rest in peace.

Alone on the Bridge of Gratitude

(A Zen Poem of Many Haikus)

I.

I've lived well and long without waiting for cell phone songs to deflect me.

II.

Appreciate death:
luxuriate in each step,
savor precious breaths.

III.

Lately, I find much
fewer eyes to meet, with these
cell phones, now replete.

IV.

Catch those vacant glares,
staring nowhere, listening:
neither here nor there.

V.

Bees are bizzy, on the go, always buzzing to and fro. Not alone!

VI.

VII.

They are the workers, makers of money, for their hives... banks of honey.

VIII.

No drone knows where it's been. Electric pulleys draw it back to the Queen.

IX.

'Star Trek' got it right:
'Borgs' and humans locked in flight:
The outcome? In doubt.

X.

Electronic swarms
with material goals, lone
critters soothing souls.

XI.

One needs leeway, time
on hold, family at bay,
brain on feline play.

The End... Almost

Finale
(in 7 Zenned Haikus)

So, has my life been
filmed illusions projected
on the cells inside

my lame brain by a
Deus ex Machina? Or
was it as a frame

through a light flashing
so quickly and unnoticed
by an audience

of all those who paid
the price to sit in judgment?
Oh, it was real. Yeah!

Every second,
every smell, every
taste, every sight.

Every choice. Each
loss was a gift from the best
producer, the best

screenwriter, the best
director souls could have
to play their best role.

About the Authors

Ted Becker has led many lives: Class clown of his high school. Sports editor of his college newspaper. Consumer researcher for a large Madison Avenue advertising agency. Member of the legal staff for the Attorney General of New Jersey. Military intelligence. Professional graduate student. Itinerant academic. Guerilla theatre producer. Boogyboarder and bodysurfer. Mediator. Online journal editor. Author of 12 books on law, politics and political science.

What about poetry? Well, it's been dormant for most of his life, but there were two previous eruptions. One came in Paris in 1964. The other in Laguna Beach, California in 1969. The third, this haiku stage, is the longest and most serious. It seems to come in waves and intensify.

Patricia Lantz is an Atlanta based counseling astrologer whose life has been an amazing journey of discovery. From the windswept prairies of Wyoming, to the coal mines and steel mills of the Ohio Valley, to the beautiful mountains and jagged shores of New England, and finally on to the steamy hot deep South... with many short stops in between... she truly considers her life to be an adventure in the human experience of living.

Patricia is also the Editor of Astrology on AllThingsHealing.com, an online community dedicated to holistic and alternative healing of mind, body, spirit and planet.

Special Offer

We hope you enjoyed and were enriched by *The Haiku Blues* in normal book form. We think of it as both a book and a work of art. However, as the latter, it can best be appreciated as such in its coffee book format. This book is 13" x 11", has a hard cover with dust jacket and has been printed on lustrous high gloss paper. It's amazing to look at and at times seems like it's in 3D. Also, it's not something you put on a shelf and forget. It will enhance your décor and constantly be within easy reach for you to go back and meditate on some of your favorites.

Given its size, heft and dazzling quality, we are offering 300 of them, a limited edition, at $295 each. If you would like to own one of these stunningly beautiful books, send a check or cash for that amount to Dr. Ted Becker, 4707 Pebble Shore Drive, Opelika, AL 36804. We will inscribe it in any way you request (that is legal and does not violate The Patriot Act), number it for you, and send it to you by FedEx or UPS. There will be a delay of about 2 weeks, since our online publisher only prints on demand and it takes at least a week before we get your copy to forward to you.

www.ingramcontent.com/pod-product-compliance
Lightning Source LLC
Chambersburg PA
CBHW042110230426
43662CB00042B/2457